A Love Letter to New Orleans

Foreword Copyright © by Soledad O'Brien, 2010

Cover Photo: ©Herman Leonard Photography LLC/CTSIMAGES.COM

Printed in the United States of America

ISBN. 978-0-578-07706-2

First Edition

5500 Prytania St. #110
New Orleans, Louisiana 70115 USA
www.BasinStreetRecords.com

www.IrvinMayfield.com

A Love Letter to New Orleans

A Love Letter to New Orleans

by
Irvin Mayfield

Foreword by
Soledad O'Brien

New Orleans, Louisiana

2011

CONTENTS

Foreword

I really got to know Irvin Mayfield around the fifth anniversary of Hurricane Katrina. I was interviewing him for a story for CNN and we were sitting in the borrowed home of a woman named Gwendolyn, who not only loaned us her living room, but also cooked up some of the best gumbo I've ever had. In true New Orleans fashion, by the end of the interview, we weren't strangers anymore. Our hour-long conversation was ostensibly about the recovery of New Orleans, but what was immediately clear about Irvin was his depth: a simple question about his musical influences triggered a conversation about politics, literature, fine art and humanity. Irvin constantly seems to be contemplating the world around him. In person, Irvin Mayfield is smart and funny, sarcastic at times, erudite and even silly--sometimes all in the same breath. There are very few people whom I consider brilliant. Irvin Mayfield is one of them. Hearing him play in the intimacy of his French Quarter Jazz club, where tourists and locals pack the house--or on the albums he has turned out for more than a decade starting at age twenty-- is to hear a multi-faceted artist exploring, examining, and forging new ground. This new compilation of fourteen songs from ten albums from the past twelve years is a treasure. "It's what I like to listen to," Irvin told me. "It's what I'd like to give people as a gift." This compilation is literally his journey as an artist. His favorite selections highlight the distance he has traveled maturing in his craft, and the distance he has traveled in miles, as he explored Haiti, Cuba, Brazil, the world. Irvin Mayfield doesn't dwell much on the past. When I asked him about the death of his father in Katrina, the storm that took so much from so many New Orleanians, he avoided the question. He said he preferred to look forward instead. Read the notes that accompany this compilation, and you discover a different side of Irvin Mayfield. He has included some of the most personal and moving comments I've ever read about his father. He is a proud father himself, passing on a musical legacy to his two young sons. Ultimately, Irvin Mayfield is an educator. He wants people to understand the complexities and nuances of New Orleans culture. He wants us to wallow in stories of heartbreak, so we can move beyond them. He captures the joy that is the essence of New Orleans, so that we can embrace it as well. Mayfield's compilation ends with *The Mardi Gras Second Line*. Listen to it as an out-of-towner, and you dream of coming back in your next life as a New Orleans native. I want them to second line when I die, too.

--Soledad O'Brien

From the author

To spend a life in music is to dedicate yourself to communicating love with people you respect and admire. You have an opportunity to get close to those whose talent inspires. Sometimes the reverse happens and you find yourself inspiring others. Music would live only in lost moments were it not for the technology of sound recording. Recordings have allowed me to embrace the golden sound of Louis Armstrong's trumpet and the rich soul of Nina Simone's voice. Mark Samuels and Basin Street Records gave me my first recording contract when I was twenty years old. Like me, Mark was also just beginning a career in the music business, and we took a chance on each other. We accomplished much together, from creating great art moments to winning many awards. We also managed to have a lot of fun. This body of work is an excerpt from ten albums and over a decade as an artist on the label. However, the thing I treasure the most from the work done with Basin Street Records is the unwavering belief in a dream that has allowed me to become the artist I am.

Irvin Mayfield
New Orleans, Fall 2010

Special thanks:

Joyce Alsanders Mayfield, Che', Irvin III, Richard, Woody, Terrence, Roemallis, Ronald Jr., Miranda, Ron III, Marty and all my family. Bill Summers, Mark Samuels, Mr. and Mrs. Kevin Poorman, the family of Herman Leonard, the family of Gordon Parks, all of the board members and staff at the New Orleans Jazz Orchestra, Dean Susan Krantz and all of my fellow faculty at the University of New Orleans, Lilly Schwartz and staff at the Minnesota Orchestra, Chairman Rocco Landesman, Alfred Groos and the Royal Sonesta Hotel.

Very special thanks:

Laura Tennyson for bringing your soul to the table, with vision and expertise in communicating the art and the brand. Freda Paz for your strategic and tactical approach to design. Jeff Strout, Greg Miles and Erika Goldring for taking thousands of great pictures. Thanks to all of the photographers, musicians, designers and audiences who participated in these projects over the years. Kim (sexy beast) Bondy for editing my words. Soledad O'Brien for your creativity. Shweta Kohsmann for your patience.

This project is dedicated to my mom Joyce Alsanders Mayfield. You have always been my inspiration, and I love you from the bottom of my heart.

Irvin Mayfield

Herman Leonard, *photographer*
1923-2010

Herman Leonard added tremendous value to the world with his beautiful, and sometimes rare, photos of musicians who dedicated their lives to upholding the legacy of the great American art form of Jazz. In 2002, Herman took the photo that graces the cover of this book and CD when he was still living in New Orleans, his adopted home. However, Hurricane Katrina devastated Herman's home and like so many others, he was displaced, and he moved to Los Angeles. I went to visit Herman at his new home in Los Angeles a month before he died. As always, he gave me advice and I gladly listened. It was there with Herman that I first really saw the outcome of the photo session we completed years before. He described the photo as powerful and sensitive. To him, the photo looked as if it had its own desire to be captured in that particular way. Herman Leonard was a legendary artist, and I feel completely honored to have shared time with him as a friend. Herman, I miss you dearly and you will stay forever in my heart.

From Basin Street Records

On March 7, 1998 in the early afternoon I was at Kinko's near the Riverbend in New Orleans making flyers for an upcoming Kermit Ruffins show, and I ran into Matt Dillon (no, not the actor). This Matt Dillon is a drummer, Wynton Marsalis' tour manager, and friend who had a show that night at the now defunct Funky Butt. We handed each other our respective flyers and he invited me to come out to his show that night.

I dozed off early that night but woke during a torrential rain and, remembering that Matt had invited me to his show, I jumped up and headed over to the Funky Butt where I caught the second set. Irvin Mayfield was performing on trumpet. At the set break I said hello to Irvin and mentioned that I had read two stories about his new band, Los Hombres Calientes -- a band that I hadn't seen, although I was familiar with his partners: Bill Summers, the amazing percussionist who had performed with everyone from Herbie Hancock to Michael Jackson to Quincy Jones, and Jason Marsalis, whom I had known since he was three years old. I was in high school band and friends with Jason's older brothers Wynton and Delfeayo, and I had spent time as a music fan with brother Branford as well. The articles I read both mentioned that Los Hombres Calientes planned to have a new record in time for Jazz Fest (the next month), so I asked Irvin how the record was coming along. He told me that he hadn't actually started working on it yet and asked if Basin Street Records was interested in putting it out. At that time we had only released one record, Kermit Ruffins' *The Barbecue Swingers Live*, and the label was still just a night and weekend hobby for me.

My business partner at the time, Tom Thompson, Irvin, Bill, Jason and I signed a contract on March 11th and started recording Los Hombres Calientes' self-titled debut on March 13th. We released that CD at the French Quarter Fest on April 18, 1998, and it was the top selling CD for two years in a row at the New Orleans Jazz and Heritage Festival. It won the Billboard Latin Jazz Album of the Year.

On the success of the Los Hombres Calientes project, Irvin signed a separate deal to release music by his modern Jazz group as well. We've done ten CDs and a DVD together. More importantly, we've traveled the world together, become friends, and supported each other through great events and tragedy. I'm proud of where he is today and expect more great things in his future. I hope this collection will give you reason to explore his Basin Street Records catalog.

Mark Samuels, Basin Street Records

A Love Letter to New Orleans

The Songs

MO' BETTER **BLUES**

Give them the love of art, they'll never lose.
Look into my soul, and you'll see the blues.

Typically, Hollywood stereotypes Jazz musicians as down-and-out men who battle inner demons and struggle to survive, sometimes both financially and physically. I have a black and white photograph, taken in 1948 by Herman Leonard, of the youthful, legendary Dexter Gordon. In the picture, Gordon sits with his polished saxophone resting on his knee and exhales a cloud of cigarette smoke which hovers above him. He looks as if he's under the spell of the blues. The photograph is one of the most famous snapshots capturing such a classic moment in the life of this well-recognized Jazz musician. When he was older, Gordon starred in the somber film *'Round Midnight*, the story of a down-and-out alcoholic saxophone player living in France who returns to New York City to play his music before tiny audiences. More recently, Clint Eastwood directed the movie *Bird*, about the tragic life of Charlie Parker. Forest Whitaker's performance as Bird demonstrated that Jazz was not a promising profession. That stereotype persisted until *Mo' Better Blues*, a movie by Spike Lee that shows the lives of Jazz musicians in a modern light. The very cool leading man played by Denzel Washington is the trumpet player, and action hero Wesley Snipes plays the saxophonist. Many fellow musicians often talk about the impact this movie had on them. It made us all believe that playing Jazz was cool and, in no uncertain terms, hip. The theme song is equally as cool and hip, and always reminds me of the time I realized I would play Jazz forever. I often end my shows all over the world with *Mo' Better Blues*. People always ask the song's name, why it's so significant to me and why I perform it so often. To me, it's more than just a song. It's my anthem.

Latin Tinge

There are two hugely successful and iconic Jazz records. The first is Miles Davis's *Kind of Blue,* released in 1959, which is often recommended for first-time Jazz listeners. The second record is Herbie Hancock's *Herbie Hancock and the Headhunters*, released in 1968. All my friends who play music have these records. Herbie Hancock's album represented the first time anyone took what Sly and The Family Stone was doing with funk and hitched it to Jazz. On the album, Herbie plays keyboard, Paul Jackson bass, Harvey Mason drums, Benny Maupin saxophone, and Bill Summers percussion. The album was Bill Summers' first recording session and it's how I first learned of him. To

New Orleans may not be geographically the

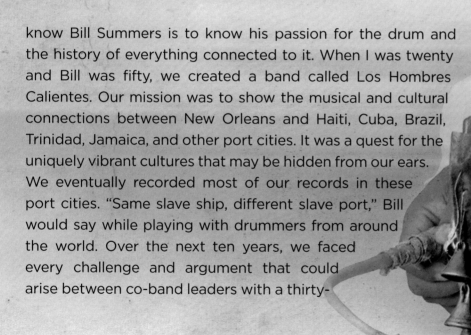

know Bill Summers is to know his passion for the drum and the history of everything connected to it. When I was twenty and Bill was fifty, we created a band called Los Hombres Calientes. Our mission was to show the musical and cultural connections between New Orleans and Haiti, Cuba, Brazil, Trinidad, Jamaica, and other port cities. It was a quest for the uniquely vibrant cultures that may be hidden from our ears. We eventually recorded most of our records in these port cities. "Same slave ship, different slave port," Bill would say while playing with drummers from around the world. Over the next ten years, we faced every challenge and argument that could arise between co-band leaders with a thirty-

he Caribbean, but culturally it certainly is.

year age difference. It was our differences, however, that made for some really diversified and energetic music. It's amazing the connections we made, and more than that, the knowledge we gained through the music. In visiting other countries that have musically influenced the world, we realized the unique role of New Orleans as a city that has cradled and nurtured Jazz to become a global musical cornerstone. New Orleans generates music with power strong enough to unfetter and awaken the human spirit, and it was through the respect and knowledge I gained from experiencing other cultures that this perspective grew. Los Hombres Calientes was my first musical passport. We don't play together often these days; however, I still believe Los Hombres Calientes' best music is yet to come.

Romeo & Juliet

When I was twenty, my heart broke into a million pieces. My girlfriend told me she was in love with another man. I tried to put every bit of hurt into this song. I don't know if I achieved my goal, but I do know for certain that it didn't provide me with any escape from the pain. Time passed, as it always does, and suddenly one day I was in a new relationship and in love. I did a themed recording around the concept of relationships. I researched all kinds of art works on the subject. There were a few representations of the good, many of the bad, and a whole lot of the ugly. But, one way or another, there is no lack of art around the subject of romance. Shakespeare's *Romeo and Juliet* is an example of man's unquenchable thirst for love, true love. Every time I hear a great Jazz ballad, it's like falling in love all over again. Ben Webster's version of *Body and Soul* will make your heart ache. Billie Holiday's rendition of *In My Solitude* will warm your soul. Ellis Marsalis' ballad performances on piano belong in the same category: his introductions like great paintings, the accompaniment like paragraphs from a great novel, the endings like final words from a dying poet. I am ever appreciative of the chance to have studied and worked alongside him. His performance of *Romeo and Juliet* will make anyone fall in love just like it's their first time.

Love is short, hurt is long. Break my heart,
I'll write you a song.

Old Time Indians

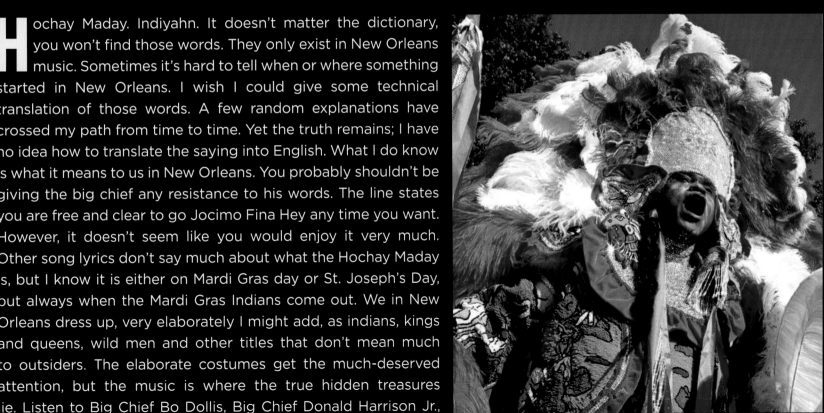

Hochay Maday. Indiyahn. It doesn't matter the dictionary, you won't find those words. They only exist in New Orleans music. Sometimes it's hard to tell when or where something started in New Orleans. I wish I could give some technical translation of those words. A few random explanations have crossed my path from time to time. Yet the truth remains; I have no idea how to translate the saying into English. What I do know is what it means to us in New Orleans. You probably shouldn't be giving the big chief any resistance to his words. The line states you are free and clear to go Jocimo Fina Hey any time you want. However, it doesn't seem like you would enjoy it very much. Other song lyrics don't say much about what the Hochay Maday is, but I know it is either on Mardi Gras day or St. Joseph's Day, but always when the Mardi Gras Indians come out. We in New Orleans dress up, very elaborately I might add, as indians, kings and queens, wild men and other titles that don't mean much to outsiders. The elaborate costumes get the much-deserved attention, but the music is where the true hidden treasures lie. Listen to Big Chief Bo Dollis, Big Chief Donald Harrison Jr.,

Cyril Neville and flag boy Walter "Dooky" Harris and you hea[r]
the rich history of our Congo Square ancestors who came from
many different areas on the globe. But the blues of the chant i[s]
undeniably American and rich with history. Neville and Harriso[n]
came together with everyday workers to record this track on a
Los Hombres Calientes album. In classic New Orleans fashion
you don't have to understand it to love it.

If you don't like what the big chief says you can Jocimo Fina Hey (Jacamo fin na n[a]

What do you call a person in New Orleans who plays the piano well? We call him Professor. There was a Creole Professor whose nickname was Jelly Roll. He was a man of the nightlife and trash talking. Jelly Roll Morton was also the first to actually write Jazz down. People all over the world recognize Professor Longhair's piano and whistle on the Mardi Gras anthem *Big Chief.* Some Professors have doctorates in gut bucket blues and funk rhythms like Dr. John. Fats Domino, simply "Fats" in the New Orleans ninth ward, was recently inducted into the Rock and Roll Hall of Fame. There are so many Professors of piano: *Moulin Rouge* songwriter Allen Toussaint; the retired Professor of Jazz Studies at the University of New Orleans Ellis Marsalis; and the great Ed Frank, who at the end of his career played better with one hand than most with two. You can also find women on the list, such as Sweet Emma Barrett, the great piano player at Preservation Hall. One of the greatest Professors of all was James Booker, an eccentric personality with a fear of the C.I.A. Despite all the distractions in his personality, his piano playing was second to none. James Booker was a flamboyant genius who turned what would be thought of as a happy-hour instrument into something imaginative, soulful and provocative. I titled a song after him because his music has taught me so much about America, New Orleans and style.

JAMES BOOKER

Everyone can't be a great artist, but a great artist can come from anywhere.

James Brooker at Jazz Fest

160F/25A

Michael P. Smith. 1978

James Booker at the New Orleans Jazz Fest   16 05/12A

Michael P. Smith, 1978

EL Negro

We're in Havana, Cuba - the old section of town. It's five o'clock in the morning and Bill Summers and I are sitting in the control booth of a recording studio. We have been in the studio since ten a.m. the previous morning. Trumpeter Elpidio Chapotin, master drummer Poncho Quinto, iconic singer Issac Delgado all say one thing to us, "Where is Negro?" Horacio "El Negro" Hernandez looks like actor Don Johnson from the T.V. show *Miami Vice*. When he plays the drums, he sounds like three of the best drummers you have heard in your life, who all have played together for a long time. If you're a drum geek, you know what I mean. I need to go no further. Music listeners would probably recognize these names: Dizzy Gillespie, who was responsible for bringing Hernandez to America,

Miles Davis and Carlos Santana, El Negro shared the stage with all of them. Born in Havana, Horacio is one of the greatest drummers in the world. We met when he replaced Jason Marsalis in Los Hombres Calientes. We immediately loved playing with one another. Playing on stage with Negro was like walking into the ancient Roman Coliseum with the biggest and baddest gladiator as your teammate. He became like a big brother to me and we got into a lot of trouble together all over the world. One of my favorite Horacio stories occurred at a San Francisco festival when its promoter bragged to Horacio and me that, while visiting Cuba, he could have paid $40.00 to sleep with women who looked like models. In response, Horacio's expression darkened with daggers in his eyes toward the promoter and he sharply said, "You, my friend, are a piece of shit." The promoter's eyes opened in shock and he uncomfortably replied, "What?" Horacio viciously shook his head and snapped, "No, no, not what? You, my friend, are a piece of shit!" The promoter weakly attempted to defend himself. I intently watched Horacio's anger rise as his eyes widened and his cheeks furiously flushed red. Horacio stopped him and reiterated, shooting his words out like bullets: "Piece...of...fucking...shit. Anyone who promotes people being exploited deserves to be called outside of their name!" he spat. The promoter sat completely still, pale white and unable to respond. I'll never forget that day. A man should never be proud of human exploitation. Horacio's rule of thumb about morality: If you couldn't confess your actions to your mother, you shouldn't be proud of them. I wrote the song "El Negro" for my friend Horacio "El Negro" Hernandez. Every time I hear this song I wonder what country he is in and what stage he is on. He deserves every note and more.

I think of myself as a citizen of the world. Music was my first passport. It took me anywhere I desired by just opening my ears.

Fatimah

Passion, Truth, Beauty and Love

It's a month before my twenty-ninth birthday. I find myself in Florence, Italy, representing the city of New Orleans as cultural spokesperson. Florence is holding events commemorating the fortieth anniversary of the city's great flood. Senator Ted Kennedy is also a keynote speaker and proverbial rock star to the Florentines because he had come to Florence forty years earlier to help rescue treasure from the flood. To say the Florentines were underwhelmed by the speaker from New Orleans would be an understatement. My first speech was doomed to failure for a couple of reasons: I did not have a formal speech prepared and Senator Kennedy went twenty-five minutes over his allotted time. The blatant yawning as I started to speak signaled something electric needed to happen. So I decided to share my experience from earlier that day when I visited Michelangelo's famous sculpture of *David*. I told them I had visited the treasured work looking for inspiration, but I thought it lacked something. No Florentine was bored at that point and the room felt as if the firing squad would soon be called in. The *David* is grand and beautiful, yet despite all of its grandeur I felt larger than the art. Every person who gazed upon *David* seemed to add something unknown to its existence. I realized Michelangelo's work was missing the same piece that all great art fails to obtain. Bringing my point into focus, I spoke on a subject all true artists know. No matter how great the artist or the work, the art itself cannot love. Only people have the capacity to love, and out of this love comes the great works of art. I love to write songs for people and I try to describe every aspect of the person through music. It's an attempt to give a musical narrative of the person's essence. Only people I deeply care about get a song, and it is very personal to me. Borrowing from the artistic perspective of the great African American artist Romare Bearden, I leave all of my pieces incomplete so the listeners can finish them. The listeners' thoughts are always my final notes.

LYNCH MOB

Slavery is always a difficult story to tell. It is often referred to as the snake that circled the leg of the table on which the Constitution was signed. This oppression through slavery, lynchings and beatings is a painful part of the American story. I believe the American story is not only one of oppression and adversity; but, if we allow the true narrative to reveal itself, it is also a story of triumph. My first real experience with the subject of lynching was as a young faculty member at Dillard University in New Orleans. I was twenty-three years old and had received a commission from the then president of the university, Michael Lomax. During a trip to Atlanta he visited the exhibit on the history of lynchings in America, *Without Sanctuary*. He was so moved by what he saw that Dr. Lomax brought a book back from the exhibit for me to read. He then commissioned a piece on the subject using the full university choir, the New Orleans Jazz Orchestra and actor Wendell Pierce as narrator. The song most talked about from the recording is entitled *Lynch Mob*. The soloist is the leader of the pack, backed up by the choir in the role of the lynch mob singing the chorus, "You better run boy run." I named the two-hour piece *Strange Fruit*, after the Jazz standard Billie Holiday made famous. One of my students recently asked me why I would make art about such a tragic topic. It is a great question about the purpose of art. Art is sometimes the only catalyst to holding a true conversation in which words can be too hurtful or distancing. Our ancestors paid the ultimate price for the generations that followed and we must never forget.

We must never forget they paid it forward for us,
they paid with their lives.

Blue *Dawn*

The dawn of life's new beginning, the secret kisses of dusk.
Love is made of the spring, we fight through the winter of us ... the blues.

"Whence did the fury come?" These are the words spoken by Wynton Marsalis. It's two o'clock in the morning in New York City, as we sit in his kitchen doing what we always do when we hang out: tell stories, recite from great works of art, laugh and talk about our home, New Orleans. Wynton has received so many awards it is mind boggling. A Pulitzer, the Legion of Honor from France, more than ten Grammy awards and, last I checked, more than twenty honorary doctorates. However, there are no awards, or pictures of famous people in his apartment. Instead, there are several chessboards and Romare Bearden's art on the walls. His home has earned the name "Hotel Marsalis" because friends from around world often stay there. He's generous in that way. Wynton loves Jazz the way the earth loves the sun, the way a note loves a practiced musician. Artistically, there is a lot of value in his sound-Louis Armstrong, Miles Davis, Freddie Hubbard are a few ingredients of his notes. New Orleans will always be the core of his sound, layered by many other cultures. When you hear him

play a long note it all adds up to be nothing less than Wynton. He plays the blues with fury. The kind of blues that Charlie Mingus talked about in the lyrics of the song that shouts, "Angel woman don't mean me no good, Needs a she-devil woman." We played the blues together many times, but mostly just for fun. *Blue Dawn* is the name of a blues I wrote late one night, thinking about my own she-devil woman. I was excited when Wynton agreed to record this blues duet with me. Judging from the sound of it, I believe Wynton's own she-devil woman might have caught up with him on a few nights too.

George Porter Jr.

My oldest son Irvin III is eight years old but could play the New Orleans beat at age six. My youngest son, Richie, is six years old and has been playing the trombone since age four. They both fell in love with George Porter's bass playing when they were just toddlers. It's hard to be a kid in New Orleans and not love George, especially when you're born into music. The iconic band The Meters was electric bassist George Porter's first entrance onto the world stage. The founding members are keyboardist Art Neville, drummer Zigaboo Modeliste, guitarist Leo Nocentelli, and bassist George Porter. They had many hits, but of course all kids love a song about the zoo. My sons not only request the Audubon Zoo song but they also love to play it. Believe me when I tell you, my kids aren't the only fans of The Meters and George Porter. They opened for The Rolling Stones for years. Ultimate jam band The Grateful Dead would

attend The Meters' concerts. Oh, and there is this thing called funk. People debate the origin of funk, but The Meters defined it as they played back up for many west coast and other national recording sessions of the time. George and I are both Capricorns but his birthday parties are a lot more fun. George is not only walking history, he's the funkiest bass player alive. He is so funky, he deserved a funky song to be named after him. You don't have to take my word for it; listen to the track called "George Porter." In other words, like another famous funky gentleman used to say, "I can't funk it for you, you gotta find the funk in yourself."

New Orleans was born funky.

Superstar

My dad would always say, "You just got here kid, you've got a long time." What I didn't realize was how short my time would be with him. Katrina brought about so much loss for my family and friends. Yet the loss of my father is still unimaginable. Maybe it's because it took so long to confirm his death. I imagine it's the feeling families have when they lose a loved one far away to war. The last project my father got to hear was a collaboration with my former instructor Ellis Marsalis. I was so excited about the recording, not just because I got to work with my former teacher, but because of the fresh standard songs and the opportunity to record with the Louisiana Philharmonic Orchestra's seventy musicians. During that time, my dad often joked about getting out his old trumpet to give me some much-deserved competition. He said it would be his retirement gig. Hurricane Katrina came and my dad perished, along with any interest in releasing the record. The failed levees destroyed all my family's photographs. I have no real pictures of my dad. One afternoon, I started to listen to the rough studio mixes that engineer Steve Reynolds downloaded into my iPod at the close of our recording sessions. All the warm memories of my dad came right back to me. I immediately called Mark Samuels at my record label and came up with a new game plan. My hopes were soon dashed when we realized what the water didn't destroy in the studio, the heat and humidity did. The albums were created from the existing recordings in my iPod and I am grateful to Steve for that. Being a musician, I often tell my sons I hear better than I see. I still miss my dad so much, but every time I hear the songs I recorded with Ellis Marsalis, my dad becomes so present. This music is now my only clear photograph of him.

The place you'll go, the people you'll meet.
Just search for you, it's a star you'll see. Keep searching.

Photographer, Writer, Film Director, Composer, Artist, and his name was

Gordon Parks

When I was twenty-two years old, the New Orleans Museum of Art commissioned me to create music based on the life work of Gordon Parks. My good friend and mentor Jonn Hankins assured me I deserved such a prestigious opportunity; after all, it was his idea. The museum provided me with every book, film and art slide they could find concerning Gordon. What I treasure most from that opportunity was getting to know Gordon Parks himself. I hear from artists, professionals and amateurs that doing something outside their comfort zone challenges them. I don't know if Gordon didn't have a comfort zone or if he just didn't care about boundaries. What I do know is that he constantly covered new territory in his work even at an age when others would have long

retired. Gordon was gifted. He didn't attend art school or apprentice under great artists. Hunger literally drove him to take his first picture in Minneapolis; advice convinced him to write his first book; curiosity led him to movie making; love and friendship spawned his first ballet. This had been all accomplished in his thirties, forties, fifties and sixties. Gordon was ninety-two when I asked if he would like to add a composition to the music I was going to record for him. He politely agreed. We were in Gordon's high-rise condominium in New York, which had sweeping views of the city's skyline. The sweet aroma of pipe smoke filled the air. Both his hands on the piano (he smoked his pipe and played at the same time, which still impresses me), he played a beautiful song he wrote for the people of New York in the wake of the September eleventh terrorist attacks. Gordon did not read music, and he told me he studied his favorite French classical composers Debussy and Ravel. When you listen to his composition *Wind Song* you can tell. Poetry is how I would describe his approach and I couldn't imagine anyone else performing this song but him. So I asked him to record it with me. He went on about how he had never done a recording session and how my piano player would be much better. I responded by saying, "But you're Gordon Parks." He looked back towards me from the piano and said, "OK old boy," as he liked to call me. I soaked up every note he played that day, and, every time I hear it, I'm brought back to the advice he gave me. Search, lead and love through your art. It will never steer you wrong.

I'LL FLY AWAY

Blessed is he who gets paid
for what he would do for free.

- Joyce Alsanders Mayfield

Every Sunday my mom made my four brothers and me go to church. We'd sit there and count the minutes until we could get home and do what we wanted before school the next day. I suppose my mother accomplished her goal because now I actually want to go to church each week. I remember a sermon I heard once when I was in Omaha, Nebraska. I like to visit different church services when I travel, and I chose an Episcopal church in this instance. The priest discussed how words are agreements and how it is necessary to come together as a community to gain better understanding of the intended agreement of the words. It made me think about language and communication. For me, music is the only art form that exists in the same space as emotion. Music is an agreement without the walls of words. Many times I hear the power of a song without even knowing the language. Words are not as powerful as tones. The tones are where the real message lies. I imagine when people hear a bunch of folks singing the church song *I'll Fly Away*, they get the same feeling I got in Havana, Cuba, watching the folks dancing and singing to Rhumba in the language of Yoruba or in Rio de Janeiro, Brazil, listening to more than a thousand people sing one melody together to proclaim they know what it means to be alive. I felt it in Istanbul, Turkey, when an old man walked down the street singing the call to prayer and everyone he crossed stopped to listen. When I decided to record this song, I asked my musical friends Cyril Neville and Davell Crawford and others to join me. I decided to add in some church folks too, like the pastor Rev. Eddie Payne and long-time church friend Franklin Davis IV. The song is the real deal New Orleans approach, and it doesn't matter if you don't know what we're singing. Just one listen and it'll wipe your soul clean.

The Mardi Gras

New Orleans is not a city. New Orleans is an opportunity: an American opportunity. It's not the music, the food, the architecture or the art that makes New Orleans great. It's the people. The ones who have gone before are just as present as the ones who are here now. I have had so many teachers of music, it's hard to name them. I have had so many great eating experiences I can't write down one sentence about them. The buildings are so diverse, it looks like the gods mistakenly dropped a pail of architectural variety on the city. Yet, the people are more powerful than all this. The people make the city come alive. They occupy a different space and a different time. The desire to document a small aspect of this amazing place musically really taught me how unique the people truly are here. Imagine this. Trumpeter and vocalist Kermit Ruffins walks in with a briefcase filled with Bud Light. Singer and songwriter John Boutte rides his bicycle to the studio. Trombone Shorty shows up with a trumpet, trombone and tuba, and plays them all. Rebirth Brass Band's Phillip Frazier, Keith Frazier, and snare drummer A.J. Mollary are in the back telling jokes. Sixth ward

Second Line

drummer Shannon Powell grabs his tambourine and tells me to hurry because "he's gotta go make some real money." Tenor saxophonist and Terence Blanchards' sideman, Brice Winston, meticulously prepares the top of his saxophone. Bill Summers is very irritated with me for having too many people in what looks like a very unorganized recording session. I wait for five more horns to show up and few additional people to make background noise. Now we are ready. Oh, I almost forgot. Wait, where is the wild man? Excited to start, I look at the chaos of the potential gumbo and scream, "Stand by! stand by!" The red recording light comes on and the Mardi Gras second line track is recorded. I promise you... that's how we do it in New Orleans.

When I die,
you better
second line.

Irvin Mayfield Basin Street Records Discography

Love Songs, Ballads & Standards
(Irvin Mayfield and Ellis Marsalis, Basin Street Records, 2008)

Strange Fruit
(Irvin Mayfield, The New Orleans Jazz Orchestra and the Dillard University Choir, Basin Street Records, 2005)

Carnival: Volume 5
(Los Hombres Calientes, Basin Street Records, 2005)

Volume Four: Vodou Dance
(Los Hombres Calientes, Basin Street Records, 2003)

Half Past Autumn Suite
(Irvin Mayfield Quintet, Basin Street Records, 2003)

How Passion Falls
(Irvin Mayfield Quintet, Basin Street Records, 2001)

Volume Three: New Congo Square
(Los Hombres Calientes, Basin Street Records, 2001)

Volume Two
(Los Hombres Calientes, Basin Street Records, 1999)

Irvin Mayfield
(Irvin Mayfield, Basin Street Records, 1999)

Los Hombres Calientes
(Basin Street Records, 1998)

Song Credits

Mo' Better Blues
Irvin Mayfield – Trumpet
Ellis Marsalis – Piano
Neal Caine – Bass
Jaz Sawyer - Drums

Latin Tinge II - Los Hombres Calientes
(with Bill Summers)
Irvin Mayfield – Trumpet Solo
Bill Summers – Percussion
Bernard Floyd – Lead Trumpets
Ronald Markham – Piano
Carlos Henriquez – Bass
Rick Sebastian - Drums

Romeo and Juliet (with Ellis Marsalis)
Irvin Mayfield – Trumpet
Ellis Marsalis – Piano

Old Time Indians meeting of the chiefs (with Cyril Neville, Donald Harrison Jr., Big Chief Bo Dolis Sr.)
Irvin Mayfield – Vocals and Arrangement
Big Chief Bo Dollis – Lead Vocals
Big Chief Donald Harrison – Background Vocals, Tambourine, and Arrangement
Walter "Dooky" Harris – Background Vocals
Geechy – Vocals and Tambourine
Cyril Neville – Bass Drum

James Booker - Los Hombres Calientes
(with Bill Summers, Carlos Henriquez)
Irvin Mayfield – Trumpet
Bill Summers – Percussion
Ronald Markham – Piano
Carlos Henriquez – Bass
Ricky Sebastian – Drums

El Negro parts 1, 2, 3 - Los Hombres Calientes
(with Bill Summers, Horacio "El Negro" Hernandez)
Irvin Mayfield – Trumpet Solo
Bill Summers – Percussion
Kent Jordan – Flute and Piccolo
Michael Ray – Trumpet
Jamil Sharif – Trumpet
Delfeayo Marsalis – Trombone
Ronell Johnson – Trombone
Edwin Livingston – Contra Bass
Ronald Markham – Piano
Horacio Hernandez – Drums

Fatimah
Irvin Mayfield – Trumpet
Jaz Sawyer – Drums
Richard Johnson – Piano
Edwin Livingston – Bass

Lynch Mob - interlude
(with Dillard University Choir)
Dillard University Choir – Vocals

Blue Dawn (with Wynton Marsalis)
Irvin Mayfield – Trumpet
Wynton Marsalis - Trumpet
Jaz Sawyer – Drums
Richard Johnson – Piano
Edwin Livingston – Bass

George Porter (with George Porter Jr.)
Irvin Mayfield – Trumpet, Wurlitzer, and Vocals
Bill Summers – Percussion
George Porter Jr. – Bass
Ronald Markham – Hammond B3 Organ
Ricky Sebastian – Drums
Philip Manuel – Vocals

Super Star (with Ellis Marsalis, Louisiana Philharmonic Orchestra)
Irvin Mayfield – Trumpet
Ellis Marsalis – Piano
Neal Caine – Bass
Jaz Sawyer – Drums
Louisiana Philharmonic Orchestra

Wind Song (with Gordon Parks)
Irvin Mayfield – Trumpet
Gordon Parks - Piano

I'll Fly Away (with Davell Crawford, Cyril Neville)
Irvin Mayfield – Vocals and Arrangement
Shannon Powell – Tambourine and Vocals
Rev. Eddie Payne – Lead Vocals
Cyril Neville – Vocals
Davell Crawford – Vocals
Philip Manuel – Vocals
Leon Brown – Vocals
Frank Davis – Vocals

Mardi Gras Second Line (with Trombone Shorty, Kermit Ruffins, Rebirth Brass Band, John Boutte)
Irvin Mayfield – Trumpet Solo and Vocals
Kermit Ruffins – Vocals and Narration
Troy "Trombone Shorty" Andrews – Trombone Solo
John Boutte' – Vocals
Che' Reed – Baritone Saxophone
Philip Frazier – Tuba
Keith Frazier – Bass Drum
Derrick Tabb "Big Sexy" – Snare Drum
Stephen Walker – Trombone
Leon Brown – Trumpet
Shannon Powell – Tambourine
Walter "Dooky" Harris – Vocals
Bryce Winston – Tenor Saxophone Solo
Rebirth Brass Band – Party Track

All compositions written by Irvin Mayfield - Irvin Mayfield Publishing BMI & Nisab Publishing BMI (except for tracks 1, 4, 11, 12 & 13)

Colophon

COVER
Herman Leonard - Irvin Mayfield portrait
©Herman Leonard Photography LLC/CTSIMAGES.COM

Greg Miles
Irvin Mayfield portrait, pg. 10
Irvin Mayfield portrait, pg. 64

Bivian (Sonny) Lee III
Herman Leonard and Irvin Mayfield
at Herman Leonard home in L.A., pg. 15

Erika Molleck Goldring
Armstrong sign, Entrance to Armstrong Park on Rampart Street
July 16, 2009, New Orleans, LA. pg. 61

THE SONGS - PHOTOGRAPHY

Mo' Better Blues
Greg Miles
*Irvin Mayfield portrait, pgs. 20-21

Latin Tinge
Jeff Strout
*Irvin Mayfield, pg. 22

*Bill Summers, Pg. 23

Bill Summers on Frenchy's mural (series), pg. 24

Bill Summers and Irvin Mayfield, pg. 25

Romeo and Juliet
Jeff Strout
*Woman on balcony, pg. 26

*still, pg. 27

Old Time Indians
Erika Molleck Goldring
Yellow Pocahontas. David Montana, 2nd Chief of the Yellow
Pocahontas, at the Bayou St. John Super Sunday,
New Orleans, LA, Sunday May 31, 2009, pg. 28

Creole Wild West. Walter Sandifer aka Hustleman of the
Creole Wild West at the Bayou St. John Super Sunday in
New Orleans, LA, Sunday May 31, 2009, pg 29

Second Line on Sunset. The Neville Brothers perform at House
of Blues October 29, 2005, in Hollywood, CA. pg. 30

Big Diva, pg. 31

Laura Tennyson
We Are Back. pg. 29

James Booker
Photo by Michael P. Smith.
©**The Historic New Orleans Collection**
James Booker, pg. 34

James Booker, pg. 35

El Negro
Jeff Strout
*Horacio "El Negro" Hernandez, pg. 36

Horacio "El Negro" Hernandez, Pg. 37

Fatimah
Greg Miles
*Irvin Mayfield portrait, pg.38

Lynch Mob
Greg Miles
*Irvin Mayfield portrait, pg. 41

Blue Dawn
Jeff Strout
*Irvin Mayfield in New Orleans setting, pg. 43

Erika Molleck Goldring
Wynton Marsalis rehearsal at Harrah's Casino August 27, 2006,
New Orleans, LA., pg. 44

Wynton Marsalis and Irvin Mayfield perform at Tulane
University January 16, 2006, New Orleans, LA, Pg. 45

George Porter Jr.
Erika Molleck Goldring
*George Porter Jr. (retouched), pg. 47

George Porter Jr. (untouched), pg. 49

Superstar
Greg Miles
Ellis Marsalis and Irvin Mayfield, pg. 51

Gordon Parks
Jeff Strout
Portrait of Gordon Parks, pg. 53

I'll Fly Away
Jeff Strout
Drum, pg. 54

The Mardi Gras Second Line
Laura Tennyson
Mardi Gras Second Line Celebration, pgs. 56, 57

Erika Molleck Goldring
Snooks Funeral 2009, pg. 58

Randy Leo Frechette aka Frenchy
Jazz Funeral Mural, pg. 59

* Photo was manipulated or altered in Abobe® Photoshop®

Art direction and book design
Freda A. Paz

Photo illustrations and photo manipulation by Freda A. Paz